1,000
Fun Facts
and
useless
information

Robby Thiele & Rick Hofmann

ISBN: 978-1-5204-3758-3

Published by Robby Thiele & Rick Hofmann, Idstein, Germany

A catalogue record for this book is available from the German
National Library

Book design by Robby Thiele

INTRODUCTION

Our world is full of miracles. Every day, so many incredible things happen, which always inspire us anew. Did you know, for example, that only five people per year die by shark attacks but 22 people by cows and even 2,900 by hippos? Who would have thought that? And who would believe that if 57 people were gathered in one room, the likelihood of two of the people having their birthdays on the same day, is about 99 percent? In our daily work for our website www.bluemind.tv, we repeatedly discovered such awesome facts and, over time, developed a certain addiction to it. Every day, we looked for more useless information and incredible facts. What we found surprised us over and over again. One fact was even more astonishing than the other, and some of them let us with doubts even weeks later. However, in the end our incredible facts are always true. Can you imagine that the entire human population could live in New Zealand, and the population density would still be lower than that of Manhattan in New York? We could not believe that and therefore checked it by ourselves. We divided the world population by the size of New Zealand and compared it to the population density of Manhattan. We recognized: incredible but true.

With this book we want to delight other people with unbelievable things facts of our world. On the following pages you will find 1,000 incredible facts and useless information with a wide range of topics. All the facts were checked by us for correctness and if you do not believe us, then take a look at our website www.bluemind.tv. On the respective website you will find even more facts and background information to many of them. We are looking forward to your visit and wish you a lot of fun with 1,000 incredible facts and useless information.

1,000 FUN FACTS AND USELESS INFORMATION

Only a few special types of piranhas eat meat. All others feed on plants.

* * *

The colder your bedroom is, the higher is the likelihood of having a nightmare.

* * *

If you close your eyes and try to walk straight, you are involuntarily inclined to walk in circles. There is currently no explanation found by scientists as to why this happens.

* * *

With a speed of 91 gigabits per second, NASA has the fastest internet-connection in the world.

* * *

The first Game Boy had as much computing power needed for the first moon landing.

* * *

An octopus has its brain in its tentacles. Even if the tentacles are separated from the body, they continue to search for food for a short time and bring them to a mouth which is no longer present.

* * *

About 83 percent of German women would abstain from sex for 100,000 Euros.

* * *

Family Guy is the first television series which, after being cancelled, came back to TV, because the DVD sales were so high.

* * *

Hugh Hefner has become almost completely deaf in recent years. Doctors believe his increased use of Viagra is the cause. Hefner however, says that he would rather be deaf than forgo sex.

* * *

A 20 second hug increases the oxytocin level of people so much that afterwards there is a much greater trust between them.

* * *

The two oldest cats in the world reached an age of 34 and 38. Both belonged to the same owner. She exclusively fed her cats bacon, eggs, broccoli and coffee.

* * *

In Spain there is a comedy club in which you pay per laugh.

* * *

Carde is the roman god for door handles, door sills and door hinges.

* * *

The inner skin of a vagina is folded and opens while having sex.

* * *

When the Big Bang theory was presented for the first time scientifically, it was rejected by many scientists because it seemed too religious.

* * *

Cleopatra was not an Egyptian, but originally came from Greece.

* * *

Apple owns more cash than the United States.

* * *

In Switzerland there are dishwashers with cheese fondue and raclette programs.

* * *

In the U.S. the most dangerous job is to be a fisherman. Approximately one out of every 900 die during work.

* * *

A study came to the conclusion that the lack of movement in the Western world kills the same amount of people as smoking does.

* * *

Butterflies are cannibals.

* * *

In China, the websites of BBC News, Amnesty International and the Dalai Lama are banned for the citizens.

* * *

At Starbucks "laughing" is part of the job description.

* * *

Each year around 1,000 people die because they are struck by lightning.

* * *

According to a study, men from Congo have the largest penises.

* * *

If you feel very connected to a person, you can hear their voice in your head when you read messages they have sent.

* * *

It is assumed that so far only four percent of our oceans have been explored.

* * *

Kenneth Bainbridge, scientific director of the Manhattan Project, commented at the first test of a nuclear bomb with "Now we are all sons of bitches".

* * *

In 2005 a used pregnancy test belonging to Britney Spears was sold for more than 5,000 dollars on Ebay.

* * *

Eight out of ten people who have been struck by lightning are male.

* * *

Some survivors of Hiroshima showed an unusual reaction. Due to the high radiation dose they were subjected to, their finger nails became black and bled slightly.

* * *

The Zoological Garden in Berlin is the largest zoo in the world.

* * *

Scorpions can survive for up to one year without food.

* * *

In the 1960s, the Barbie model "Slumber Party Barbie" was released, which gave children extra tips on how to lose weight. One of them was that you should not eat anything.

* * *

"Nomophobia" describes the fear of not being available via mobile phone.

* * *

Every 21st inhabitant of New York is a millionaire.

* * *

Blind people are able to dream and to see pictures in their dreams.

* * *

Ioannis Economou, the chief translator of the European Parliament, speaks 32 languages fluently.

* * *

During the 19th century in the UK, the sentence for an unsuccessful suicide attempt was death by hanging.

* * *

In Asian culture, white is a mourning colour. Therefore Asian wedding dresses are never white.

* * *

Living in the White House is not free for the President of the United States. He receives a monthly bill for food and other expenses.

* * *

In 1856 a man from Havana took off in his hot air balloon and was never seen again.

* * *

Translated into Spanish "Colgate" means "hang yourself".

* * *

Just one percent of all heart attacks is caused by sex whereas ten percent are brought about by getting up too fast.

* * *

It is possible to die even 24 hours after drowning. People who die from "dry drowning" do not tend to notice their discomfort while the water continues to spread in their lungs until they die.

* * *

The actor Robin Williams was passionate about video games, which is the reason why he named his daughter "Zelda".

* * *

Because of the large amount of sugar in it, it is impossible for honey to spoil. Even in 1,000 years it would still be edible.

* * *

The Sagrada Familia in Barcelona has been under construction for over 130 years and is still not finished.

* * *

The westernmost point of the USA and the easternmost point of Russia lie just three miles apart.

* * *

Pumba from "The Lion King" was the first Disney character who was allowed to fart.

* * *

In 2012 a British man named Wesley Carrington bought a metal detector and within 20 minutes found gold from the Roman Age worth 100,000 pounds.

* * *

Women who frequently play video games have more sex than other women.

* * *

At the Marine Mammal Studies Institute, dolphins have been trained to get the audiences waste out of the basin. Each time they hand out trash to the animal attendants, they get food for it.

* * *

After James Cameron saw Star Wars for the first time in 1977, he quit his job as a truck driver and began his career in the film industry.

* * *

Slugs are able to sleep three consecutive years.

* * *

Neither Hollywood nor Bollywood produced the most movies per year. It is Nollywood in Nigeria, where about 2,000 movies are finished a year.

* * *

Goosebumps are a reflex from the times when man had much more hair. When our hair stands up, we appeared bigger and more menacing to enemies.

* * *

In 1985, a school child named Ryan White was not allowed to attend class because he had AIDS. About 117 parents and 50 teachers signed a petition for this. Some parents even ended their newspaper subscription, as Ryan White was their paper boy and the believed they could get infected.

* * *

Toilet paper was invented in China in the 13th century.

* * *

From a water depth of 33 feet and more there is no more red light. For this reason blood seems to be green at this depth.

* * *

One bite of the Inland-Taipans - the most poisonous snake in the world - injects enough poison into its victim to kill more than 230 people.

* * *

There is a type of jellyfish which is immortal.

* * *

The first call with a mobile phone was made by its inventor, Martin Cooper. He called a rival to brag about his achievement.

* * *

Although the Incas had a huge empire, they did not possess money. The inhabitants paid their taxes in the form of man power and got food in exchange for this.

* * *

In 2006, scientists officially declared that the egg came first, not the chicken.

* * *

The Vatican has its own telephone company, its own radio station, its own TV station, its own stamps, its own money and its own army.

* * *

The penis foreskin of burn patients can be used for healthy skin growth.

* * *

Swans only have one partner in their lifetime.

* * *

The longest distance at which a sniper has killed his target is 2,707 yards. The bullet flew through the air for a total of six seconds.

* * *

At a height of almost 12 miles and above the air pressure is so low, that water in your body would vaporize due your own body temperature.

* * *

In Amsterdam there is a gym where you can train naked.

* * *

Before coffee became popular, beer was served for breakfast in the USA.

* * *

A study proved that men really have problems understanding women's feelings.

* * *

GTA originally was meant to be a racing game named "Race'n'Chace" but a glitch made police cars ram into the car of the player. This element was so popular with the game testers that a whole game was modelled on this principle and GTA was born.

* * *

If one donates a part of one's liver, the missing part will grow again.

* * *

Frederic Baur developed the boxing of Pringles Chips. After his death in 2008, his ashes were buried in a Pringles box.

* * *

At the beginning of the 20th century, horses created so much dirt with their excrement, that cars were regarded as the "green" alternative.

* * *

An average cloud weighs about 1.5 million pounds.

* * *

The starting melody of Windows was composed on a Mac.

* * *

After Steve Jobs' secretary was late due to her car breaking down, he later that afternoon gave her the keys to a new Jaguar, and told her, "Here, don't be late anymore."

* * *

Wildlife goldfishes can live up to 40 years.

* * *

When James Cameron was in a Roman hospital due to food poisoning he had a nightmare about a robot from the future trying to kill him. From this idea he created the script for "Terminator".

* * *

Contraceptive pills also work for gorillas.

* * *

When the Egyptians built the pyramids, there were still mammoths roaming the earth.

* * *

In terms of the number of museums, theatres and libraries, Germany is the country with the most opportunities for cultural activities.

* * *

Monhar Aich won Mr. Universe in 1952. Today he is more than 100 years old and exercises regularly at the gym.

* * *

In 2009, Marc Aurus - an expert on the prevention of kidnapping - gave a lecture on the topic of "How to avoid being kidnapped in Mexico" and was then kidnapped.

* * *

In the special edition 3 of the Club Nintendo comic book series, the reader finds out that Kirby smokes, drinks and eats unhealthy fast food.

* * *

A study has shown that four percent of all people dream exclusively in black-and-white.

* * *

The average distance a man walks on foot during his life is four times around the world.

* * *

About 99,99999999999% of an atom is "nothing". If one would eliminate the empty space of all atoms from the entire human race, the remaining mass would fit in a coffee mug.

* * *

Redheads are less sensitive to pain and more sensitive to temperature when compared to people with different hair colors.

* * *

The production cost of one penny is 1.7 cents.

* * *

Foxes use the Earth's magnetic field to estimate distances.

* * *

The first hard disk for Apple II had a capacity of five megabyte.

* * *

The author J. K. Rowling was the first person in the world who became a billionaire by selling books.

* * *

Panama is the only country in the world in which the sun rises above the Pacific Ocean and sets over the Atlantic Ocean.

* * *

In Austria there are three toilets, which are listed for preservation.

* * *

Since 1896, soccer fields in Germany have to be free of trees.

* * *

George Washington was known to convince voters with the help of alcohol. At an election campaign with over 400 people, he brought over 500 liters of alcohol to secure their votes.

* * *

New York is located more southern than Rome.

* * *

Each year a lying competition takes place in England. Participants have to tell a made up story for five minutes. To be "fair", politicians and lawyers are not allowed to participate.

* * *

In Iran 70 percent of all science students are female.

* * *

Renfield-Syndrome is characterized by an obsession with drinking blood.

* * *

So far about 270 people have had their bodies frozen, to be revived in the future.

* * *

The croissant is not a French creation, but an Austrian creation.

* * *

The Scottish kilt originally came from France.

* * *

The Tammar wallaby has a weight of only one gram at birth.

* * *

A study has shown that people with a lot of body hair have on average a higher IQ than people with less body hair.

* * *

On average, first-borns have the highest IQ among their siblings.

* * *

From 1781 to 1850, the planet Uranus was named George.

* * *

In ancient Rome the punishment for rapists was their genitals being smashed between two stones.

* * *

Costa Rica does not have its own military anymore. Instead, the money is now spent on education and culture.

* * *

Ransom payments to abductors can be written off as taxes in Germany.

* * *

It is impossible to draw a six while turning your foot clockwise simultaneously.

* * *

Alaska crosses the border with the eastern hemisphere and is thus the most eastern and western state in the USA.

* * *

Currently, there are about seven billion people on earth who make experiences and memories every day. A total of 220 years of new human memories are generated per second.

* * *

Depending on the cause of crying, tears have a different chemical composition.

* * *

Starbucks was named after the first mate of Captain Ahab in Moby Dick.

* * *

In the Middle Ages green was the colour of love.

* * *

Sleeping on your belly can lead to crazier, creepier and more sexual dreams.

* * *

The word "gym" comes from Greek and translates to "place of the naked."

* * *

The "Big Ben" has its own Twitter account with 450,000 followers. Every hour a new tweet with "Bong, Bong, Bong" appears, whereby the number of "bongs" varies with the hour.

* * *

Golf balls were originally made of wood.

* * *

In ancient Greece the sandals of prostitutes bared an inscription, so that the words "follow me" appeared on the sandy ground.

* * *

Babies can already get an erection in the womb.

* * *

The full name of Mr. Burns is Charles Montgomery Plantagenet Schicklgruber Burns.

* * *

Left-handers on average live longer than right-handers.

* * *

The medical term for headaches due eating to ice-cream is sphenopalatine ganglioneuralgia.

* * *

The Cookie Monster from Sesame street is actually named "Sid"

* * *

In London the buses are red because the owner wanted to stand out from the competition.

* * *

Pizza is one of the few words that is understood almost everywhere in the world.

* * *

Gottfried Svartholm, a co-founder of Pirate Bay, let his mother read instructions for using computer programs to him at the age of six, in order to learn the basics of programming.

* * *

The reflex that we automatically lead a small wound to our mouth is an innate protective mechanism. The saliva in our mouth helps the blood to coagulate and kills bacteria.

* * *

From a statistical point of view, women are the better drivers, as they cause less accidents.

* * *

In Iceland, two-thirds of all university graduates are female.

* * *

The phenomenon that people forget things which are easy to look up on Google, is called the "Google Effect".

* * *

In 1913, Adolf Hitler, Joseph Stalin, Leo Trotsky, and Sigmund Freud all lived close to each other in the immediate vicinity of Vienna, and regularly went to the same cafe without ever having come into contact with each other.

* * *

There are the same amount of chickens and humans on Earth.

* * *

Although Clint Eastwood smokes in almost all of his movies, he himself is not a smoker.

* * *

Gandhi was nominated five times for the Nobel Peace Prize, but never received it.

* * *

The first server at Google was built from legos.

* * *

Cats sweat through their paws.

* * *

The vagina has a self-cleaning mechanism.

* * *

A fifth of all people use their smartphone during sex.

* * *

The second name of Richard Nixon was Milhouse.

* * *

In the 17th century, New York was called New
Amsterdam.

* * *

In the 1940s, the Coca Cola Company developed a
colorless version of Coca Cola specifically for the USSR.

* * *

The Golden Gate Bridge is made up of so many wire
ropes that put together they would circle the earth three
times.

* * *

A man on average gets eleven erections per day. Nine
during his sleep.

* * *

NASA plans to grow crops on the moon in the next six
years.

* * *

In 1906, the physicist J. J. Thompson won the Nobel Prize for his proof that electrons are particles. 31 years later his son also received the Nobel Prize for his proof that electrons are a wave.

* * *

Since 1964, in memory of the victims of the atomic bomb, the "flame of peace" is burning in Hiroshima, which will only be extinguished once all nuclear weapons on the earth have been eliminated.

* * *

In India, 45 percent of all residents have a mobile phone, but only 30 percent have access to a toilet.

* * *

Since 2013, every citizen of Uruguay is allowed to buy 40 grams of marijuana at a pharmacy for their own personal use. Due to the good price of one dollar per gram, as specified by the state, many former drug lords have left the now unprofitable drug business.

* * *

If you bathe in alcohol, you can get drunk.

* * *

Only two percent of the human population has green eyes.

* * *

Frank Oz, the voice of Yoda in Star Wars, was also the voice of Miss Piggy.

* * *

An average pubic hair has a life expectancy of three weeks. A head hair "lives" in comparison up to seven years.

* * *

According to a U.S. study, marriages between homosexual couples are less likely to lead to divorce when compared to marriages between heterosexual couples.

* * *

When cows eat too many carrots, their milk can turn pink.

* * *

The human is the only mammal which cannot swallow and breathe at the same time. We lose this ability when we start talking.

* * *

The development of chemical drugs can be traced back to the Nazis. For example, scientists in the Third Reich discovered an active substance that helped soldiers to march 55 miles without stopping.

* * *

The Italian "San Marino" is the oldest republic in the world.

* * *

To protest against mechanization during the Industrial Revolution, workers threw their wooden shoes into the machines. This is how the word "sabotage" was born.

* * *

In 2010, General Electrics made profits of 14 billion dollars and paid not a penny in taxes.

* * *

You can't commit suicide by holding your breath.

* * *

Pornhub once started campaign called "Save the Boobs". For every 30th view in the category "small tit" or "big tit", the company donated one penny to the "Susan G Komen Foundation" - a foundation whose aim is to cure breast cancer. However, the foundation refused the donation. Therefore, Pornhub tripled the amount of money and donated it to a foundation with a similar purpose.

* * *

The "S" in the name of Harry S. Truman only represents an "S".

* * *

In the U.S. state of Minnesota, a three-year-old was mayor for a short time.

* * *

To kill a spider, a woman in Kansas burned down her house.

* * *

Four percent of all people do not fold their toilet paper, but scrunch it together instead.

* * *

In the USA, there is a sports league for rock-paper-scissors competitions.

* * *

The Foreign Accent Syndrome describes a disease in which the affected persons involuntarily speak their mother tongue with a foreign accent.

* * *

If you enter "Beam me up, Scotty" as a search term on YouTube, all videos are "beamed" to the screen.

* * *

When Hitler visited during World War Two, activists cut the elevator cables of the Eifel Tower so that he had to climb the stairs all the way to the top.

* * *

Pierce Brosnan was contractually prohibited from wearing suits in other films during his time as James Bond.

* * *

In Iceland, Greenland and the Antarctic there are no ants.

* * *

If you start counting from one, then 1,000 is the first number in which the letter "A" occurs.

* * *

The most frequently visited tourist attraction in Paris is not the Eiffel Tower or the Louvre, but Disneyland.

* * *

A bite of the Brazilian wandering spider can cause men an erection that lasts for hours.

* * *

The inventor of the Gameboy was initially a janitor at Nintendo.

* * *

In Turkey there is a city called "Batman".

* * *

Laughing one hundred times burns the same calories as a 15-minute workout on the bike.

* * *

In 2010 a pizza was sold for 10,000 Bitcoins. At today's exchange rate this would be four million dollars.

* * *

The actor Morgan Freeman has already been nominated for more prizes than he has made films.

* * *

On average, there are 88.8 weapons per 100 U.S. citizens.

* * *

There is a programming language called ArnoldC, which consists only of quotes by Arnold Schwarzenegger.

* * *

In Finland every traffic ticket is based on your personal income. The highest fine ever paid for speeding was 100,000 Euros.

* * *

The shoe size of the Statue of Liberty is size 879.

* * *

The world record for wearing the most underpants at the same time is at 302 pairs.

* * *

O. J. Simpson was freed, among other things, because it was proved that the investigator was biased. In a telephone conversation, he mentioned the word "Nigger" more than 40 times.

* * *

Vikings took cats on sea trips in order to avoid a rat problem. Nowadays, it is assumed that this prevailed the worldwide spread of cats.

* * *

Each year about 100 million bikes are produced worldwide.

* * *

Each year, about one million new employees are hired by McDonald's in the U.S.

* * *

The human eye reacts so well to light that it could see the flame of a candle in absolute darkness from about 30 miles away.

* * *

Koala bears, monkeys and humans are the only animals with an individual fingerprint.

* * *

In the 18th century the Briton Mary Toft became famous for giving birth to rabbits. Years later she was sentenced to death when it became clear that she just put dead rabbits in her vagina, which she pushed out later on.

* * *

During the nine seasons of "How I Met Your Mother" Ted dated 29 women who were not the mother.

* * *

The honor code of comic book authors forbids the use of werewolves in comics.

* * *

When the Cornhuskers - the football team of the University of Nebraska- have a home match, the stadium becomes the third biggest city in the state.

* * *

"Bart Gets an F" - the first episode of the second season of "The Simpsons", is the most viewed Simpsons episode.

* * *

According to Bill Gates, just a small amount of poor countries will exist in 2035.

* * *

An average U.S. citizen consumes as many resources as 32 people in Kenya use during the day.

* * *

In 1987 American Airlines was able to save 40,000 dollars because they used one less olive in their salads.

* * *

Students get better test results when looking at a green landscape during the test.

* * *

Corals are chemically so similar to human bones that they are used to treat fractures.

* * *

So far, there have already been around 106 billion people in the world.

* * *

At the beginning of the 20th century, radium was often used as an ingredient in facial cream.

* * *

In Minneapolis, Minnesota, a room has been developed, for research purposes, that absorbs all sounds. If you are inside, it is so quiet that you can even hear your own pulse. However, if you stay too long in absolute silence, hallucinations may occur.

* * *

Similar to the fingerprint, each human has an individual tongue print.

* * *

Polar bears are left-handed.

* * *

Jim Cummings, the voice of Winnie Pooh in the U.S., regularly calls seriously ill children in hospitals and talks to them in his Winnie Pooh voice to delight them.

* * *

The sign "Made in Germany" was originally intended to warn British people of inferior items from Germany.

* * *

The Golden Gate Bridge has to be painted regularly. The salt water corrodes the paint so fast, that one has to start repainting the bridge as soon as one is finished painting it.

* * *

In 2013, more people died in the United States from children playing with small guns then from terrorists

* * *

Leonid Rogozovy is the only human to do an appendectomy with local anaesthesia on himself.

* * *

Humans and dolphins are the only animals, which have sex solely for pleasure.

* * *

John Adams, the second president of the United States once said "I have come to the conclusion that one useless man is called a disgrace; that two are called a law firm; and that three or more become a Congress!"

* * *

A study from 2002 showed that 60 percent of people cannot have a ten minute conversation without having lied at least once.

* * *

Scientists assume that the face of the Sphinx was painted red.

* * *

Rice has more genes than humans.

* * *

The original name of "Bank of America" was "Bank of Italy".

* * *

In Japan, there is an office tower in which a highway runs though, between the fifth and the seventh floors.

* * *

Ryan Gosling was short-listed to be in the Backstreet Boys.

* * *

Thanks to a language computer, Stephen Hawking can speak at a rate of one word per minute.

* * *

The real name of actor Michael Keaton is Michael Douglas.

* * *

Cats cannot taste sugar.

* * *

Instead of "LOL" people in France say MDR for "mort de rire", which means laughing to death.

* * *

In Australia in 2009, snipers were tasked with defending a colony of penguins against possible enemies to guarantee the survival of this rare penguin species.

* * *

The letters "J" and "Q" do not occur in the periodic table of elements.

* * *

George Lucas obtained the rights to the word "droid". When Motorola released a cell phone with this name, they had to pay a fee to George Lucas.

* * *

In ancient Babylon it was tradition for every woman to go to the Temple of Aphrodite at least once in her life to have sex with a stranger.

* * *

The first flags of pirates were red, not black.

* * *

The gravity on the moon is about one-sixth of the earth's gravitational pull.

* * *

It is impossible to cause your own death by strangling yourself.

* * *

The names of the main characters in the film "Inception" are Dom, Robert, Eames, Arthur, Mal and Saito. When you combine the initial letters of these names, you get the word "Dreams".

* * *

In 1980 a hospital in Las Vegas had to dismiss several employees as they were betting on when patients would die.

* * *

To protect the German soldiers from the British night vision technology, they spread the lie that eating lots of carrots helped British soldiers to increase their eyesight during night. A myth was born.

* * *

On average, each major character of "How I Met Your Mother" earned 120,000 dollars per episode. Barney Stinson actor Neil Patrick Harris earned 210,000 dollars per episode.

* * *

The record for "The most orgasms in one hour" is 134 for women and 16 for men.

* * *

The national animal of Scotland is a unicorn.

* * *

Walt Disney has received 63 Oscar nominations throughout his lifetime, of which he has won 26. Thus, he is the world record holder of most Oscar wins.

* * *

If you salt a pineapple, it tastes sweeter.

* * *

In New Zealand, there is a lake, which on average has a temperature of 147 degrees Fahrenheit due to geothermal processes.

* * *

The Islamic movement "Moro Islamic Liberation Front" calls itself "MILF".

* * *

Hans Zimmer has composed the soundtracks for "Lion King", "Gladiator", "Pirates of the Caribbean", "Inception" and for the "Dark Night" trilogy. According to him he spent two weeks in a music class during his childhood and learned the rest by himself.

* * *

During the Olympic Games in China, Usain Bolt ate only chicken nuggets, as it was the only meal he recognized from home. Ultimately, he won three gold medals with this diet.

* * *

When Einstein heard of the book "100 Authors Against Albert Einstein," he replied, "Why 100? If I were wrong, one would be enough."

* * *

Spending more than 15,000 dollars for a wedding increases the rate of divorce compared to couples who have a cheaper wedding.

* * *

The average age of soldiers fighting in Vietnam was 19. During World War II it was 26.

* * *

A short nap after studying helps the brain to remember the materials studied better.

* * *

It is impossible to sneeze with your open eyes.

* * *

The role of the character Captain Jack Sparrow from "Pirates of the Caribbean" was originally given to Jim Carry. He refused as he rather wanted to make Bruce Almighty.

* * *

Koalas sleep about 90 percent of their lives.

* * *

There is no physical description of Jesus in the Bible.

* * *

Dolphins sleep with there eyes open.

* * *

The teeth of limpets are the hardest biological material in the world.

* * *

In 1981 a hard disk containing one gigabyte cost 300,000 dollars.

* * *

Scientists believe they have discovered an evolutionary jump. It was discovered that the Australian lizard stems from an egg-laying species to a viviparous one.

* * *

The word "alphabet" consists of the words "alpha" and "beta", which are the first two letters in the Greek alphabet.

* * *

Based on statistics, the best drivers have the zodiac sign Leo while the worst drivers are Taurus.

* * *

Annually, more people die from being hit by a champagne cork than from the bite of a venomous spider.

* * *

According to a survey conducted in 2000, Japanese people think that instant noodles are the greatest Japanese invention of the 20th century.

* * *

Vagina is the Latin word for "sheath".

* * *

In war times significantly more boys than girls are born. This is called the "Returning Soldier Syndrome".

* * *

Although woman are permitted to become pilots in Saudi Arabia it is prohibited for them to drive a car.

* * *

Months beginning with a Sunday always have a Friday 13th.

* * *

Around 35 percent of all billionaires have never graduated from higher education.

* * *

Did you know that the the brain hides superfluous information, like the second "the" in this sentence?

* * *

The average person watches their favorite movie 29 times in their lifetime.

* * *

In the early 50s a "Blow Job" described the bang when breaking the sound barrier.

* * *

The first cloned cat has been called "CC" as an abbreviation for "carbon copy'".

* * *

In biological terms, love is an addiction. The serotonin level among lovers is as low as among drug dependents.

* * *

Big Ben is only the name of the main bell in the belfry of London. The correct name of the bell tower is "Clock Tower".

* * *

A Jamais-vu is the opposite of a Déjà-vu.

* * *

Reading reduces your stress level much more than listening to music or walking.

* * *

To date, about 5,000 people have already turned their ashes into an artificial diamond after death.

* * *

At birth, the blue-whale baby is already 23 feet long and weighs more than two tons.

* * *

As the earth rotates more slowly around the sun from year to year, 2016 was one second longer than 2015.

* * *

The U.S. channel Fox has the rights on the Simpsons until 2082.

* * *

Sweden has the least amount of murders each year.

* * *

If one took all the world's water and placed it into a cube, it would accommodate 39,375 cubic feet.

* * *

When the game "Twister" was released in 1966, it was described as "sex in a box".

* * *

There are about nine million people in a prison around the world. 25 percent of them come from the USA.

* * *

Listening to music is the only activity which involves all areas of the brain.

* * *

With one pencil, one is able to draw a line with a length of up to 37 miles.

* * *

The combination of a knife with a fork and a spoon is called spork.

* * *

Due to reduced air pressure, water on Mount Everest boils at 158 degrees Fahrenheit.

* * *

Barney Stinson from "How I met your Mother" is the real inventor of the "Bro-Code". Based on Google search analytics the term hadn't existed before 2008.

* * *

In France it is prohibited by law, to name a pig
"Napoleon".

* * *

Central Park in New York is larger than the State Monaco.

* * *

In the U.S., a man stole several million dollars after having
beaten a security system consisting of security guards,
infrared sensors, motion detectors and a safe door. He was
arrested when DNA traces were discovered on the
remainders of a sandwich that was found in a trash can
next to the crime scene.

* * *

Water only gets the typical chlorine smell when someone
pees in the basin.

* * *

In one second an average two people die.

* * *

Tibetan monks sleep while sitting.

* * *

Rabbits have such good peripheral sight they are able to
see things behind their head.

* * *

To prepare for her tour, Beyoncé always sings while jogging.

* * *

On average a man ejaculates about 7,000 times in his life.

* * *

A nap of six minutes at midday improves memory capacity significantly.

* * *

Before she became famous, the singer "Pink" worked for McDonald's.

* * *

In Stockholm Sweden, there is a pilot project, which involves receiving an SMS when someone has a heart attack nearby and the ambulance has been called. Then the receiver can rush to the location and execute a heart lung massage. So far 9,500 people have joined this project and in 54 percent of the cases, people reach the location before the ambulance and are able to provide assistance.

* * *

The largest cat in the world had a length of 1.36 yards.

* * *

The cactus "Saguaro" can grow up to 20 feet tall and live for over 300 years.

* * *

Seen chronologically, Cleopatra was closer to the moon landing than to the construction of the pyramids.

* * *

Brryan Jackson's father infected his son with HIV at the age of eleven months to kill him, because he didn't want to pay alimony. Within 5 years the doctors diagnosed AIDS in Jackson. They gave him just a few months. Today, Brryan Jackson is 20 years old and HIV has not been detected in his blood for more than five years.

* * *

Women blink more frequently than men.

* * *

The first name of Master Yoda from Star Wars is "Minch".

* * *

If you enter "= rand ()" in Microsoft Word, you get a random text.

* * *

In 1957 a senior woman had to be brought out of a baseball stadium after being hit in her face by a baseball. When the paramedics were carrying her out, a second ball hit her.

* * *

The capital of Kazakhstan is Astana. Which when translated means "capital".

* * *

Alcohol protects against radiation.

* * *

Australia exports camels to Saudi Arabia.

* * *

The "Medical Students Disease" describes the phenomenon of medical students suffering from the disease they recently have learned about in class.

* * *

The first seven seconds are the most important when making a first impression.

* * *

The people who voiced Mickey Mouse and Minnie Mouse in the 1930s were married in real life.

* * *

When it comes to extreme heat in Melbourne, the lions in the zoo are given frozen blood.

* * *

It takes 40 minutes to cook an ostrich egg.

* * *

The average income of an intern at Facebook and Snapchat is between 8,000 to 10,000 dollars a month.

* * *

There is a Barbie doll which is modelled after Angela Merkel.

* * *

The human circadian rhythm is better suited to life on Mars than on Earth.

* * *

The slogan of Vermin Supreme, a candidate for the U.S. presidency, was "Free ponies for all Americans".

* * *

In medieval France, women were among others punished by being forced to catch a chicken in the city while naked.

* * *

Most accidents at work happen on Mondays.

* * *

The song "Hey ya" by Outkast says "Shake it like a Polaroid picture", forced Polaroid to release a press release that shaking a Polaroid too much can damage the picture.

* * *

Worms can have up to ten hearts.

* * *

If. There. Is. A. Period. After. Every. Word. Our. Brain. Automatically. Starts. Making. Pauses. After. Each. Word.

* * *

The area on earth, which is suitable for coffee plants to grow, is called the bean belt.

* * *

"Broken Heart Syndrome" is the medical term for the separation of a beloved partner. The symptoms can be so strong, that the patient gets cardiac dysrhythmia, suffers from pain and is not able to breathe properly.

* * *

Germany was the first country to implement summer time.

* * *

The most economically unprofitable movie in U.S. history is "ZYZZXD Road". It earned a total of 20 dollars.

* * *

Bob Marley's song "No Woman No Cry" was actually called "No Woman Nuh Cry". This song is not about the better life of men without women, but about the life of a sad woman.

* * *

Babies already dream in their mother's womb.

* * *

After a 19 year old girl became the three millionth follower of Venezuelan President Hugo Chávez on Facebook, the president gave her a house.

* * *

Everything you write into your Facebook status, is irreversibly sent to Facebook - regardless if you actually post it.

* * *

On a flight from Amsterdam to Boston a woman from Uganda gave birth to a child. In the end, the baby was given Canadian citizenship as it was born in their airspace.

* * *

Sneezing too intensively can cause a broken rib.

* * *

In Lapland, the horns of reindeers are sprayed with reflective color so that they can be seen better in the dark and car accidents can be prevented.

* * *

In 1976 the BBC made an April fools hoax, that the planets in our sun system are located in a special constellation so that the gravity is decreased. This resulted in more than one thousand calls, confirming that one actually can feel the effect.

* * *

A pineapple was such a large status symbol in 18th century England that you could rent it for a day.

* * *

The most common words in the world are "ok" and "cola".

* * *

Canada has more lakes than any other country in the world.

* * *

The former U.S. politician Thomas Jefferson believed that every law should automatically become void, to be replaced by a new law, which is adjusted to the new generation.

* * *

More than 50 percent of the world's population has never received a phone call.

* * *

Bangladesh, although just one percent the size of Russia, is more populated.

* * *

In Pittsburgh there is a restaurant called "Conflict Kitchen". It only serves dishes from countries the USA is in conflict with. When the restaurant started to serve dishes from Palestine the owners received death threats.

* * *

The release of the film "The Princess and the Frog" led to more than 50 cases in the US where children were infected with a disease because they had kissed a frog.

* * *

High heels were originally worn by men to look taller. It was only in the 17th century that women began to wear such shoes in order to be more masculine. The result was that men were no longer wearing high heels, so as not to look feminine.

* * *

The human is the only primate who has no bone in his penis.

* * *

Sea water has an average salt content of 3.5 percent.

* * *

When leaving school, a child in the U.S. has already witnessed 40,000 people dying on TV.

* * *

The first car accident with fatalities happened in 1896 at a speed of less than four miles per hour.

* * *

During his time in school Isaac Newton wrote an essay on how water moves from the roots to the leaves in a tree. This phenomenon could first be scientifically proven about 225 years later.

* * *

With every ejaculation a man unloads one to two teaspoons full of sperm.

* * *

In eight cities in Italy, an elevated level of cocaine and marijuana in the air can be documented.

* * *

Because of pressure balance it is impossible to whistle in a space suit.

* * *

People who own iPhones have sex more often compared to Android users.

* * *

The word "Swagger" is a neologism and was created by William Shakespeare.

* * *

In the history of Mexico, on one occasion, there were three presidents on one day.

* * *

Grapes explode when you heat them in a microwave.

* * *

The election slogan "Yes we can" actually comes from "Bob the Builder".

* * *

Because all passports in UK are officially issued by the Queen, she does not own a passport. When travelling abroad she just has to state that she is the Queen.

* * *

In the nineties, 50 percent of all CDs produced were the free AOL Internet CD.

* * *

In order to prevent tickets to his concerts becoming too expensive, musician Kid Rock charges a maximum of 100,000 dollars per gig.

* * *

Martin Goodman - one of the founders of Marvel - thought Spider-Man was a bad idea because people do not like spiders.

* * *

During the making of the film "Star Wars - Return of the Jedi Knights" a number of crew members surrounded the actor playing Chewbacca in forest scenes to guarantee his safety. They were afraid that hunters might think he was Bigfoot.

* * *

Scientists assume that the first human who will reach 150 years old or older, has already be born.

* * *

Adolf Hitler was nominated for the Nobel Peace Prize in 1939.

* * *

The city with the longest name in the world is Llanfairpwllgwyngyllgogerychwyrndrobwllllantysiliogogog och and is located in Wales.

* * *

The founder of "Victoria's Secret" sold the company for a million dollars in 1982 and committed suicide in 1993 by jumping off the Golden Gate Bridge.

* * *

Johnny Depp always has his Jack Sparrow costume while travelling and visits children in hospitals regularly as Captain Jack Sparrow.

* * *

When the first telephones came people answered there call with "ahoy".

* * *

The spider species "Caeristris darwini"spins the largest webs in the world. Their size can reach more than ten feet.

* * *

Jonas Salk refused to take out a patent on his polio vaccine. He commented that: "There is no patent. Could you patent the sun?"

* * *

Researchers in Australia are working on a new condom made of cellulose that is 30% thinner but 20 percent more robust.

* * *

Eminem's mother sued the rapper because he insulted her several times in his songs. She received damages of 1,600 dollars.

* * *

Diabetic patients are unable to regulate their blood glucose level. For this reason, the glucose level is sometimes so high that even the urine of a diabetic patient would taste sweet.

* * *

Rock Bottom Remainders is a music band in which Simpsons creator Matt Groening and book author Stephen King are members.

* * *

Peanuts are not nuts but in fact beans.

* * *

Although women's brains are slightly smaller, they are more efficient then men's brains.

* * *

Okinawa Island in Japan is the safest place in the world. More than 450 people, who are more than 100 years old, live there.

* * *

Scientists have demonstrated that cats have the same brain patterns as humans have during sleep. It is therefore assumed that cats can dream.

* * *

In China there is an app where you can order a "gangster", who can take care of your "enemies".

* * *

Male ants have no fathers because unfertilized ant eggs always produce male ants and only fertilized eggs produce female ants.

* * *

Before the actor James Franco became successful, he practiced different accents while working as a cashier at McDonald's to see his customers reactions.

* * *

The actor Nicolas Cage has already purchased his own grave. It is a pyramid several meters high in New Orleans.

* * *

Stephen Hawking has now surpassed the life expectancy estimated by doctors by 50 years.

* * *

Microsoft sued the student Mike Rowe after he launched the site MikeRowSoft.com.

* * *

Genetically, mushrooms are closer to humans than to plants.

* * *

French was the national language of Great Britain for more than 300 years.

* * *

There is no law in Denmark which prohibits breaking out of jail.

* * *

Octopi have three hearts.

* * *

Pandas become more fertile when they watch other pandas having sex. For this reason, pandas watch "Panda Pornos" in zoos to increase their fertility.

* * *

Before McDonald's offered burgers, the company sold hot dogs.

* * *

The International Space Station is the most expensive object ever made by humans. It has cost 160 billion dollars so far.

* * *

In Cambridge (Canada) you can pay your parking ticket by donating soft toys.

* * *

The sign on the entrance of the town Kurt Cobain was born in, reads "Come as you are".

* * *

Taiwan was the first country to provide free Wi-Fi to all citizens.

* * *

In Italy on New Year's Eve, traditionally one wears red underwear to have luck for the new year.

* * *

Before there were trees on the earth, our planet was covered by giant mushrooms.

* * *

Due to global warming, the sea level rises by approximately three millimeters each year.

* * *

According to NASA, Jurassic Park is the seventh best movie in the world, measured in terms of scientific accuracy.

* * *

The holes in Swiss cheese are called "eyes". A Swiss cheese without eyes is called "blind".

* * *

In 1994 the iPad would have been the fastest computer on earth.

* * *

Every year around 600 lightning bolts strike the Statue of Liberty.

* * *

All faces we see in our dreams are faces of people we have already met in real life.

* * *

Most serial killers are born in November.

* * *

In Ireland for a long time it was tradition that one liter of Guinness beer was given for each liter of donated blood.

* * *

Leonardo da Vinci loved animals so much that he often bought caged animals to set them free.

* * *

The Sims was originally designed as an architecture simulator.

* * *

By his 13th birthday, Mike Tyson had already been arrested 38 times.

* * *

The original name of the movie "Scream" was "Scary movie".

* * *

In its language selection, Facebook offers the language "pirate".

* * *

If you Google "elgooG", you will get to a mirrored Google.

* * *

Approximately eight percent of human DNA is from the DNA of viruses that infected humans thousands of years ago.

* * *

People with creative professions have higher life expectancies than people with other professions.

* * *

The name "Google" is derived from the word "googol" which denotes a one followed by one hundred zeros.

* * *

The fear of long words is called hippopotomonstrosesquipedaliophobia.

* * *

Pigs cannot see to the sky.

* * *

During "How I Met Your Mother" there have been 13 interventions. The most popular ones were Barneys frequent usage of magic tricks, Marshals addiction to charts and Lilly's fake British accent.

* * *

Because the movie "Psycho" was produced in black-and-white, chocolate syrup was used for blood.

* * *

Based on a fan petition, LEGO launched the production of a special Big Bang theory set in 2015.

* * *

The reason why actor Morgan Freeman wears earrings is due to a maritime tradition. They wore their earrings, so that their own burial could be paid with them, in case of their death.

* * *

If you Google "241543903" you get numerous pictures of people who have put their heads in the refrigerator.

* * *

Chinatown in New York is the largest settlement of Chinese citizens outside Asia.

* * *

The chimpanzee "Congo" was able to draw abstract works of art. Even Pablo Picasso was a fan of his pictures.

* * *

The 100 richest people in the world earned so much money last year that they could end global poverty four times over.

* * *

A newborn just has 234 milliliters of blood in its body.

* * *

On average, people laugh ten times a day.

* * *

In 1911, the Niagara Falls froze completely.

* * *

A study from 2003 came to the conclusion that French
people, among all nations, have most frequent sex.

* * *

Family Guy is prohibited in the following countries:
Indonesia, Iran, Vietnam, Taiwan, Egypt, South Africa,
South Korea and Malaysia.

* * *

According to estimates, the iPhone is the most profitable
product in the world. About 50 percent of the selling price
is Apple's profit.

* * *

The first person shooter "Half Life" has already been
successfully used in the treatment of arachnophobia (the
fear of spiders).

* * *

People cry the amount it would take to fill one bath tub in
their whole life.

* * *

From water depth of 33 feet and more it becomes
impossible to fart.

* * *

The table tennis ball in "Forrest Gump" was inserted by special effect designers, so that Tom Hanks never had to play table tennis.

* * *

Because of a reduction in the emission of greenhouse gases, scientists predict that the ozone hole will close in 2075.

* * *

Schools test only your memory and not your intelligence.

* * *

Nutella has a sun protection factor of 9.5.

* * *

Edgar Bergen was the first man to win an Oscar made of wood for his ventriloquial performance.

* * *

In Dubai people own refrigerator magnets, which order a pizza by pressing them.

* * *

The DNA among humans differs by just 0.1 percent. In comparison, a chimpanzee is genetically different from humans by 1.2 percent.

* * *

A normal person can distinguish up to one million colors. Approximately three percent of the female population can, however, perceive over 100 million different colors due to an additional photoreceptor in the eye.

* * *

In 2009, a ten year old tried to sell his grandma on eBay.

* * *

Because of their extremely hairy chest the "Hasselhoff crab" was named after David Hasselhoff.

* * *

In Japan, it is socially acceptable to sleep while working. It is perceived a sign of hard work.

* * *

Michael Jackson proposed a Harry Potter musical, but J. K. Rowling refused.

* * *

It takes the sun 226 million years to circumnavigate the Milky Way.

* * *

According to a survey from 2008, about 58 percent of British teens believed that Sherlock Homes really existed.

* * *

Dubai uses falcons to keep their cities free of pigeons.

* * *

A human could survive two minutes in space without a space suit.

* * *

Only eight percent of the world's money is physical. The rest exists digitally.

* * *

The website "godtube.com" describes itself as YouTube for Christians.

* * *

In Iowa, a 99 year old senior woman sews one dress every day to donate them to children in Africa.

* * *

British woman Wendy Southgate is most commonly seen on Google Street View.

* * *

The cousins of Sailor Moon are Sailor Uranus and Sailor Neptune.

* * *

In 2010 a professor at the Kansas State University wanted to show his students that during a diet only the amount of calories is important, and not the nutrients. For two months he almost exclusively ate candy and lost more than 26 pounds.

* * *

On average, a man ejaculates 7,200 times during his entire life.

* * *

An iPad with apps installed weighs more than an iPad without apps installed.

* * *

Zebras and ostriches often stay together in the wilderness. Ostriches can see enemies at long distances, while zebras are able to hear enemies from far away.

* * *

On the distant planet HD 189733b it rains molten glass at wind speeds of 4,350 miles per hour.

* * *

The founder of Wikipedia - Jimmy Wales - has only a fortune of about one million dollars.

* * *

In 1967, a former Prime Minister of Australia disappeared without a trace and has still not been found.

* * *

Playing video games increases creativity, concentration and makes you happier.

* * *

About 60 million people who are alive today, will die within the next 12 months.

* * *

When the Mona Lisa was stolen from the Louvre in 1911, Pablo Picasso was one of the suspects.

* * *

With total assets of approximately 500 billion dollars, "Black Panther" is the richest superhero in the world, much richer than Batman (about 80 billion dollars) and Iron Man (about 100 billion dollars).

* * *

If you have a ten dollar note in your pocket and do not have any debts, you are richer than 25 percent of U.S. citizens.

* * *

Because it was impossible to transport the ingredients needed for Coca Cola in Nazi Germany, the Coca Cola Company designed a beverage especially for the German market: Fanta.

* * *

When the pirate Jean Lafitte learnt of a bounty on his head of 500 dollars was issued by the governor, he issued a bounty on the governor's head of 5,000 dollars.

* * *

Based on current extrapolations Bill Gates could be the first trillionaire in the world.

* * *

Eggs can explode in the microwave.

* * *

Sperm contains only five calories. So it only gets you fat when you are pregnant.

* * *

The two most common reasons for a bad temper are hunger and insufficient sleep.

* * *

The dance style "Daggering" was forbidden on Jamaican television, as it lead to numerous penis fractures during the dancing.

* * *

Beards have a health-benefit effect. They prevent pollen from entering the mouth so that the possibility of getting hay fever is decreased.

* * *

The vaginal fluid of women can be found in sharks.

* * *

When Google shut down for five minutes in 2013, the world internet traffic decreased by 40 percent.

* * *

If you hold a grain of sand against the night sky, it will hide 10,000 galaxies from your eyes.

* * *

In France people were killed by the guillotine up until 1977.

* * *

The word "Tsundoku" is Japanese and describes people who buy many books but never read them.

* * *

McDonald's is not the largest restaurant chain in the world. Subway is.

* * *

Between 2011 and 2013, McDonald's has opened one branch a day in China.

* * *

According to current estimates, it would cost more than 23 billion dollars to build a real "Jurassic Park".

* * *

When two wolves mate, they stay together for the rest of their lives.

* * *

If a man would never shave his face, his beard would be approximately 30 feet long on the day he dies.

* * *

The least people are born in February.

* * *

People with red hair are more resistant to anesthetics.

* * *

In India there are milkshakes with marijuana.

* * *

If Coca Cola was served without colorants, it would be green and not black.

* * *

The glass globe above the German Reichstag building symbolizes that politics should always be transparent and that the people stands over the government.

* * *

Jabbar Collins was imprisoned for 16 years. During this time he read numerous law books and found a procedural error which led to his freedom and a compensation of ten million dollars.

* * *

The word "mafia" refers to the criminal organization in Sicily. Comparable structures in other regions use their own names like "Camorra" or "Yakuza".

* * *

In 1970, roughly six billion dollars was spent on fast food. Nowadays, it is about 200 billion dollars.

* * *

In 1995, Newsweek published an article in which it expressed the opinion that the Internet would never make it. Meanwhile, this article is available on their website.

* * *

From 1789 to 1790, New York was the capital of the USA.

* * *

Cats are the most popular pet in the United States. There are 88 million cats compared to 74 million dogs.

* * *

In the movie "Halloween" the villain Michael Myers wears a mask. In order to save production costs, they bought a Captain Kirk mask and simply painted it over.

* * *

Since 2010, Google has bought on average one company a week.

* * *

Pac-Man was originally named "Puck Man"

* * *

It is genetically determined whether you can role your tongue or not.

* * *

It would require 1,200,000 mosquitoes to exsanguinate the blood out of a human.

* * *

Henry Ford was the first tycoon to not let his employees work on Saturdays and Sundays, so that they could spend more time with their cars. Thus the weekend was born.

* * *

There are just two people who know the recipe for Coca Cola. For this reason they are not allowed to be in a plane at the same time.

* * *

In an online petition, 87,000 people voted for McDonald's to serve a vegetarian burger.

* * *

On the small island of Limone sul Garda in Italy the inhabitants have developed a genetic mutation that makes it impossible for them to have a heart attack.

* * *

In Uganda there is a kingdom called Buganda and its national language is Luganda.

* * *

The younger you look for your age, the higher the likelihood to live for a long time.

* * *

If you write "3:)" on Facebook you will see a little surprise.

* * *

Since 1987 Starbucks on average opens two stores a day.

* * *

Instead of using lawn mowers, Google has about 200 goats that graze the grass on the Google site.

* * *

The most common first name in Italy is Russo.

* * *

There is a woman whose name is actually "Marijuana Pepsi Jackson".

* * *

On average, children start lying at the age of four.

* * *

People with blue eyes have a higher tolerance threshold for alcohol and are therefore drunk only after consuming larger quantities of alcohol.

* * *

The construction of the Titanic cost seven million dollars. The film starring Leonardo DiCaprio cost 200 million dollars to produce.

* * *

Star Trek was the first TV series to show a kiss between a white man and a black woman on TV.

* * *

In 1972 the first black superhero to get his own comic book series, Luke Cage was released.

* * *

For fun, a British couple invited the Queen to their wedding. The Queen actually came to the wedding.

* * *

On the occasion of the new Star Wars Movie "The Force Awakens" the weirdest products were sold under the "Star Wars" trade mark. Including a knife block, oranges, mascara and special "Yoda water".

* * *

Penguins can jump six feet high.

* * *

After the first drive-in was opened at McDonald's in China, the system was so strange to the Chinese people that many people ordered their food from their car, parked their vehicle and then went to the restaurant to eat.

* * *

Shakuntala Devi holds the world record in mental arithmetic. In 1980 a computer randomly chose the two 13-digit numbers 7,686,369,774,870 and 2,465,099,745,779, which Devi had to multiply. It took her only 28 seconds for the correct answer: 18,947,668,117,995,426,462,773,730!

* * *

During a press conference in the 70's a reporter asked Stevie Wonder, what it was like being born blind. He answered "It could have been worse. I could have been born black."

* * *

Three men from Yemen accused NASA for "settling" on Mars. According to the men, their ancestors gave it to them 3,000 years ago.

* * *

About 90 percent of all lung cancer cases are caused by smoking.

* * *

The shortest commercial flight lasts only 47 seconds and brings people in Scotland from the Westray Island to Papa Westray Island.

* * *

Female kangaroos have three vaginas.

* * *

During the production of "Toy Story 2", an employee accidentally erased the whole movie and almost ruined the production. Fortunately, one of the employees had a backup on her desktop computer, so the work went on and the movie made it to the cinemas.

* * *

After Josef Stalin had heard that his son failed to commit suicide, he said: "He can't even shoot straight."

* * *

The deepest hole ever explored by man was 7.5 miles deep. Compared to that, the earth has a diameter of 7,926 miles.

* * *

Fingernails grow approximately four times faster than toenails.

* * *

One side effect of aspirin is headache.

* * *

According to Amazon, the best-selling books on Kindle are the Bible, the Steve Jobs biography and the Hunger Games trilogy.

* * *

Facebook also allows for exotic smileys. If you write (^^^) as a comment a shark appears. With <(") you see a penguin and: poop: creates a small pile of poop.

* * *

A blowjob under water is called "Aquabob".

* * *

Approximately 70 percent of the world's total oxygen is released by plants in the oceans.

* * *

One gram of DNA contains as much information as could be stored on 600 billion traditional CDs.

* * *

Scientists believe that it is possible to exterminate all mosquitoes, without impacting on our global ecosystem.

* * *

The seven wonders of the ancient world only existed concurrently for 60 years.

* * *

Japanese people believe that black cats bring good luck.

* * *

Scientist support that on Enceladus, a moon of Saturn, streams of water can be found.

* * *

A "moment" is a medieval time unit, exactly 90 seconds. An hour therefore has 40 moments.

* * *

Celery has "negative" calories - it costs more energy to digest it.

* * *

In South Africa there is a bar in a 6,000 year old tree.

* * *

Einstein believed that mankind would only survive four years after the extinction of bees.

* * *

The longest sentence in a book can be found in "Les Miserable". It consists of 823 words.

* * *

When Erich Honecker, a GDR politician, first visited the Federal Republic of Germany, his red carpet was 8 inches shorter than usual, because the Federal Republic did not want to show him the same respect as other citizens and friends.

* * *

Timothy Ray Brown is the first man to be cured from AIDS. In 2007 he received a bone marrow transplant due to his blood cancer. After the treatment, doctors could not detect HIV in his body anymore. To date, nobody knows how this was possible and whether the disease will come back. This phenomena could only be detected on two further people.

* * *

More than 800 castles are currently on sale in France.

* * *

The more intelligent one is, the more zinc and copper can be found in one's hair.

* * *

The 2022 World Soccer Championship will be opened in Lusail (Qatar), a city which did not exist till recently.

* * *

If classical music is played in wine shops, the turnover increases by 2.5 times compared to the wine shops where pop music is played.

* * *

The speculum - a tool for gynaecologists - was already used 1,300 years before Christ.

* * *

To investigate in a strip club in Seattle, an undercover agent visited the club 160 times and spent 16,835 dollars of tax payer money for at least 130 lap dances. Currently not one single person has been charged in this case.

* * *

For blind people, who are allergic to dog hair, there are blind horses. A special breed, who are extremely small and very tame.

* * *

For car races, Nissan only uses the number 23 on their vehicles, since in Japanese number two is pronounced as "ni" and three as "san". Together this gives "ni-san".

* * *

The 1996 Nokia Communicator was the first ever smartphone, it cost 800 dollars and even had a fax connection.

* * *

In Norway, you pay half the amount of normal tax in December, to have more money for Christmas.

* * *

About 20 percent of all calories consumed worldwide comes from rice.

* * *

In preparation of the movie "Rocky" Sylvester Stallone asked the former professional boxer Earnie Shavers to beat him multiple times in the face at full force. Stallone vomited after his first punch.

* * *

Muhammad Ali is the only famous person whose star on the "Walk of Fame" is not on the sidewalk itself but on the wall of a building. He did not want people trampling on his name.

* * *

A nap improves your memory and protects against heart disease.

* * *

An anonymous donor pays for the college tuition of each student in Kalamzoo, Michigan.

* * *

While the mortality rate for cancer ten years ago was 215 deaths per 100,000 people, it has subsequently decreased to 172.

* * *

In 2012, the CEO of Lenovo received an annual bonus of three million dollars. Instead of keeping the money for himself, he distributed it among his 10,000 employees.

* * *

One million seconds correspond to about twelve days, but one billion seconds correspond to 32 years.

* * *

E.T. was originally a horror movie, in which aliens reach the earth and kill humans by touching their heads with their fingers.

* * *

Only nine percent of consumers of marijuana are addicted.

* * *

As the water of a coconut is isotonic and sterile, it is used as saline solution in underdeveloped countries.

* * *

Bushes and clouds in Super Mario Bros have the same shape, only the color is different.

* * *

In 539 BC the Persian king "Cyrus the Great" adopted the first human rights of the world. He thus freed all slaves and gave people the right to decide for themselves what they wanted to do.

* * *

Due to more accurate methods in GPS surveying, the official size of Liechtenstein in Europe was corrected by 10,760 square feet in 2014.

* * *

Most board games are sold in Germany.

* * *

The place with the lowest gravitational pull is in Canada.

* * *

The Candlefish is so oily, that it used to be burned and used as a candle.

* * *

In Turkmenistan, water, gas and electricity has been free to citizens since 1991.

* * *

In 1647 Christmas was forbidden by the English Parliament.

* * *

About 89 percent of all men have problems with differentiating between kind behavior from a woman and flirting.

* * *

Ötzi suffered from lactose intolerance.

* * *

When the first railroads started to operate, doctors warned of health effects, such as in the brain. This was due to its high speeds of up to 19 miles per hour.

* * *

In the 1960s, a female fan hid in postal package and was sent by a friend to the Beatles' address. The postal services however, discovered and freed the lady before she was able to be posted.

* * *

The IKEA catalogue is the only book on earth, of which there are more copies than the Bible.

* * *

Octopus-Wrestling was a popular trend in the sixties. A diver grapples with an octopus in shallow water and tries to bring it to the surface.

* * *

Coca-Cola owns the websites ahh.com, ahhh.com and so on. The website with the longest URL contains 62 "h"s.

* * *

Female skunks are able to influence the development of their embryos, in order to delay birth in times of food shortages.

* * *

In 1893, a U.S. citizen made an application to change the name of the country to "The United States of the Earth".

* * *

In 1999 the founders of Google wanted to sell their company to one of its biggest competitors "Excite" for one million dollars but were rejected.

* * *

In France it is not prohibited to marry a dead person.

* * *

In the 1890s Bayer, a pharmaceutical company in Germany, advertised heroine as a medicine.

* * *

The oldest high-school graduate in Germany is 73 years old.

* * *

It is unknown where Mozart was buried.

* * *

By licking a postage stamp, you consume 0,1 calories.

* * *

In Germany, almost each second marriage ends in divorce.

* * *

There was already McLobster, McSpaghetti and McPizza, on offer at McDonald's.

* * *

Lake Karachay in Russia has been overrun with so much nuclear waste after World War II, that one hour of exposure is a lethal dose of radiation.

* * *

It takes an average employee at McDonald's about seven months to earn the amount the CEO makes in one hour.

* * *

In 1958 an atomic bomb disappeared from the arsenal of the U.S. Army in Georgia. To this day it has not been found.

* * *

Night vision devices display a green image because people can perceive the most amount of contrast in green.

* * *

Gray whales exclusively mate in a threesome.

* * *

After watching the series "Breaking Bad", Hannibal actor Anthony Hopkins wrote a letter to Bryan Cranston, the main character of the series, and told him: "Your performance as Walter White was the best acting I have seen - ever".

* * *

The dress that Princess Diana wore on her wedding with Prince Charles had an 26 feet long train.

* * *

When a Fiat employee realized when the Google Street View car will record Södertälje in Sweden, he parked a Fiat in front of the Swedish Volkswagen headquarter to be present in Google Street View for the next years.

* * *

The thermometer was invented in Italy.

* * *

If you twist both index fingers very slowly in a clockwise motion and then move them faster, the circles suddenly move in the opposite direction.

* * *

During the day, clouds fly higher than during the night.

* * *

Mothers instinctively kiss their newborn baby. Through the kiss the mother takes up bacteria and viruses of the child and forms antibodies which can pass through the mother's milk to the child.

* * *

If you could fold a piece of paper 42 times, that piece of paper would be able to reach the Moon.

* * *

Liliy's high school lover, Scooter from "How I Met Your Mother", is the husband of Barney actor - Neil Patrick Harris - in real life.

* * *

Rome holds the world record for the city with most elevators.

* * *

The human heart beats more than 100,000 times a day.

* * *

The modern look of the U.S. flag was designed by a school child from Ohio as a school project. His teacher gave him a B-.

* * *

To date, 43 Germans have won an Oscar and 81 have been awarded the Nobel Prize.

* * *

In order to avoid a long-standing dispute, the CEO's of Southwest Airline and Stevens Aviation decided to resolve their problem by arm wrestling. The winner was given the right to use a specific advertising slogan.

* * *

The Swedish man Max Martin is the most successful music composer in the world. Among others he wrote the songs "Wish You Were Here", "Quit Playing Games With My Heart", "I Want You Back", "Oops! ... I Did It Again", "It's My Life", "Since U Been Gone", "I Kissed a Girl", "Hot n Cold", "Dynamite", "DJ Got Us Fallin' in Love" and "Fucking Perfect".

* * *

On average, German women have their first baby at the age of 29.

* * *

Studies have proved that an increase in the amount of homework correlates with the increased likelihood of students to become depressed.

* * *

The intelligence of a child is primarily determined by its mother.

* * *

In 2009 in Florida, a man who was accused of owning child porn, said his cat had downloaded the files.

* * *

There are more people with obesity than malnutrition worldwide.

* * *

Approximately 20 percent of the French landmass is outside of Europe. For example the islands Martinique and Guadeloupe are in the Caribbean Sea.

* * *

Pandas are able to fake a pregnancy to get more food from the zookeepers.

* * *

On January 1 1985, the first phone call was made using a cellular phone.

* * *

Nintendo means "temple of heavenly responsibility".

* * *

Before English became the dominant language in the U.S., German was the second most common language.

* * *

The album "Hybrid Theory" by Linkin Park is the most sold debut album of the 21st century.

* * *

The deepest gold mine in the world is located in South Africa, and is situated 2.5 miles below the surface.

* * *

On the basis of number of viewers, Disney's Jungle Book was the most successful movie in Germany.

* * *

The founders of Adidas and Puma were brothers.

* * *

Monowi in Nebraska has only one inhabitant and he is also mayor of the city.

* * *

90 percent of people start fake laughing when they do not understand what others have said.

* * *

Only three years after the first football rules were laid down, the hand play was forbidden.

* * *

Chris Putnam is a developer at Facebook and has immortalized himself in social networks. If one writes :putnam: in a comment, one will see his face as a smiley.

* * *

Because people born blind smile from birth, scientists have concluded that smiling is a genetically determined behavior which is not learned.

* * *

All people begin their lives as females. The male Y chromosome becomes active just after the fifth week of gestation.

* * *

One study documents that many people, after two years of obtaining their tertiary qualifications, remember only ten percent of the content they have learned.

* * *

It is impossible to pinch your nose and say "Mhhh" for more than three seconds.

* * *

In Italy, Lazio policemen drive Lamborghinis.

* * *

The movie "French Kiss" is called "English Kiss" in France.

* * *

The first successful blood transfusion took place in 1660 and was between two dogs.

* * *

In 1968 Kip "Keino" almost arrived late to the Olympic 1,500 meter run, due to a traffic jam. He therefore left the car, ran the remaining 2.5 miles to the stadium and took home the gold medal.

* * *

In the state prison of Indiana, the occupants may keep cats.

* * *

According to FIFA, the five meter space of a football field must be 5.50 meters wide.

* * *

Men more frequently dream of other men, while women dream of both sexes equally.

* * *

The superhero Flash is faster than Superman.

* * *

The oldest ever found advertisement dates back to 3,000 BC and was found in the ruins of Thebes. It advertised a slave named Shem.

* * *

Because intelligent people think faster, their handwriting is sloppier.

* * *

In summer, storks poop on each other's feet in order to cool down.

* * *

There area road systems where music is played when a car drives at the right speed.

* * *

Netflix has over 20 million subscribers in China even though Netflix is not available in China.

* * *

A statistician at Standford University has already won the lottery four times and has received over 20 million dollars.

* * *

Between 2009 and 2012, Alexander Bychkow killed and ate at least nine people. According to him, he did this to impress his ex-girlfriend, who had ended the relationship prior to the killings.

* * *

The term "money laundering" can be traced back to Al Capone, as he used Laundromats for this purpose.

* * *

In 1879 the Belgian mail service launched a pilot project in which cats were used to deliver the letters. The project failed.

* * *

When McDonald's opened a restaurant in Rome in 1986, demonstrators handed out free pasta to counter McDonald's fast food.

* * *

A phenomena referred to as the "CSI effect" explains when jurymen become influenced by television series such as "CSI Miami".

* * *

On average, a raindrop reaches a speed of 21.7 miles per hour.

* * *

J. K. Rowling - the author of the Harry Potter books - is no longer a billionaire. She has donated most of her fortune.

* * *

In the USA, a slave from 1850 by today's standards, would cost 1,000 dollars.

* * *

Mars is the only known planet which is inhabited solely by robots.

* * *

Pirates wore an eye patch, so they could take it off at night and so could see better in the dark.

* * *

There are more public libraries in the U.S. than McDonald's restaurants.

* * *

In space you cannot burp.

* * *

Termites eat their food at double the speed when heavy metal is played.

* * *

Genetically, humans possess the requirements for hibernation.

* * *

Saddam Hussein had a Koran, written with his own blood.

* * *

In 2008, a female shark gave birth to a pup without having been previously fertilized. So far there are only two cases of asexual reproduction of sharks worldwide.

* * *

In Texas, there is a city called Earth; it is the only place in the world named "Earth".

* * *

The Greenland shark, among others, eats polar bears and deer.

* * *

The majority of astronauts, U.S. Presidents and Nobel Prize winners were first-borns.

* * *

Approximately 96 percent of all French secondary schools have condom vending machines on their grounds.

* * *

450 men die of cancer in the U.S. each year.

* * *

Approximately 200,000 new people are born each day.

* * *

Angela Merkel's middle name is Dorothea.

* * *

Sharks and rays are the only animals that cannot develop cancer.

* * *

In the movie "Pulp Fiction" all clocks show the same time: 4.20 o'clock.

* * *

The highest ever documented weight of a human being was 1,400 pounds.

* * *

The designer Ko Yang has invented a milk package that changes its color when the milk begins to spoil.

* * *

Human gastric acid is so corrosive that it could dissolve a razor blade.

* * *

About 75 percent of all people are scared of speaking publically in front of people.

* * *

Humans are the only species that cook their food.

* * *

The official title of the British Prime Minister's cat is "Chief Mouser to the Cabinet Office".

* * *

Even during the night there are rainbows. They are called "moon bows".

* * *

If you visit Rainymood.com you can hear the sounds of rain.

* * *

A study proved that 70 percent of women prefer to eat chocolate rather than have sex.

* * *

Miguel Indurain, five times Tour de France winner, has a resting heart rate of 28 beats per minute.

* * *

The drug lord Pablo Escobar had so much cash in his home that rats ate about a billion dollars of his wealth per year.

* * *

Vin Diesel invested 3,000 dollars to produce the film "Multi Facial". The film was about his problems getting a real major role. Steven Spielberg watched the movie and cast Vin Diesel for his first major role in "The Soldier James Ryan". From then on his career began.

* * *

All Scandinavian countries have a cross on their flag.

* * *

More people know the logo of McDonald's than the Christian Cross.

* * *

In 2005, Mark Zuckerberg offered Facebook for 75 million dollars to MySpace. The CEO of MySpace, Chris DeWolfe - declined.

* * *

The weirdest things that have been found in food sold by McDonald's are: bandaging material, the head of a chicken and a dead rat.

* * *

The Jewish boxer Salamo Arouch was imprisoned in a concentration camp during World War II and was forced to fight against other inmates. The loser was shot or gassed.

* * *

The police of Saudi Arabia have a special witches-unit, where people can report cases of magic. Fortune telling is also considered a crime.

* * *

The most common fracture in the human body is the collarbone.

* * *

Around 75 percent of all vehicles, which were produced by Rolls-Royce, are still in operation.

* * *

David Hasselhoff secured the rights to his nickname "The Hoff" and the phrase "Do not Hassel the Hoff" as part of his divorce settlement.

* * *

While tomatoes are typically classified as vegetables, they actually belong to the fruit category.

* * *

Because a big butt is a sign of fertility, men feel more attracted to women with larger butts.

* * *

The longest beard ever measured on a woman had a length of 10 inches.

* * *

Besides Steve Jobs and Steve Wozniak there was a third founder of Apple: Roland Wayne. He sold his shares in 1976 for 800 dollars.

* * *

Most books stolen in German universities are legal books. The second most commonly stolen books are books with a theological background.

* * *

According to nutritional values, the daily requirement of vitamin B6 can be provided by 1.3 kg Nutella.

* * *

In 1954 Bob Hawke, the future prime minister of Australia, set the world record by drinking 2.5 liters of beer in 11 seconds.

* * *

The first president of Zimbabwe was President Canaan Banana.

* * *

A study came to the conclusion that women are more attractive to men when they do not use make-up.

* * *

The oldest bar in Ireland, which still exists, was opened 900 years before Christ.

* * *

Because emus and kangaroos are not able to walk backwards, they are officially referred to as heraldic animals.

* * *

The Wall of China cannot be seen from space - however, China's smog can.

* * *

The X-Men No. 1 is the best-selling comic book in the world with a total of eight million copies sold.

* * *

In terms of stress levels people aged 18-33 face the hardest challenges.

* * *

Tsutomu Yamaguchi was working in Hiroshima when the first atomic bomb hit the city. As he was driving home to Nagasaki the second bomb hit. He is currently 90 years old and still alive.

* * *

A study concluded that people with a lower IQ more frequently tend to be more homophobic and racist than people with a higher IQ.

* * *

In 200 million years, a day on Earth will last 25 hours.

* * *

James Fixx, the creator of the word "jogging" died from a heart attack while jogging.

* * *

A person has between 100,000 and 150,000 hairs on their head.

* * *

The silk of the spider species "Caeristris darwini" is the toughest biomaterial in the world - ten times stronger than a comparable strand of Kevlar.

* * *

Regular sex can relieve nasal congestion and help treat asthma and hay fever.

* * *

Your mouth contains more bacteria than your anus.

* * *

Strawberries are not berries, but in fact nuts.

* * *

Because of the reduced distance to the central core of the earth at the equator, people at the equator weigh less than people at the poles.

* * *

The more you burp, the less you have to fart.

* * *

If all the gold in the world was melted, a dice with an edge length of 66 feet would be the result.

* * *

To prove their credibility in court in early Rome, men have sworn on their balls.

* * *

When the space probes Rosetta and Philae left the earth on March 2, 2004, there were no iPhones, Facebook existed for 27 days and nobody knew of Twitter.

* * *

In the history of the United States there have been 17 Americans who ran a marathon in less than two hours and ten minutes. In October 2011 this was achieved by 32 Kenyans.

* * *

In remembrance of the deceased actor Paul Walker, Vin Diesel named his daughter "Pauline".

* * *

NASA claims it will be able to answer the question if we are alone in universe in the next 20 years.

* * *

It took one year to sell a million copies of the first iPhone. With the iPhone 6, a million copies were sold on the first weekend of its release.

* * *

Since the end of the Second World War, Japan has apologized in official statements more than 50 times for its acts during the war.

* * *

George Washington was known to spend approximately seven percent of his annual salary on alcohol.

* * *

In Estonia, Wi-Fi is made freely available to all citizens - even to the 90 percent who live in the forests.

* * *

In 1930 Ketchup was sold as medicine.

* * *

The average depth of the oceans is 2.5 miles.

* * *

The average price of one liter of black ink is higher than the price of one liter of human blood.

* * *

After being hit by an avalanche, the arctic scientist Peter Freuchen freed himself by making a chisel from his frozen stool. After this, he amputated his frostbitten toes with a hammer.

* * *

After the death of Leonardo da Vinci, King Franz I. of France hung up the Mona Lisa in his bathroom.

* * *

Falling asleep next to a loved one helps one to doze off faster and decreases the risk of depression.

* * *

Facebook is blue because the founder Mark Zuckerberg suffers from red-green color blindness.

* * *

Being in love releases the same hormones that the use of cocaine releases.

* * *

There is no city that is more often destroyed in movies than New York.

* * *

Tom Hanks brother - Jim Hanks - sounds very much alike his brother, which is why he occasionally does synchronization work for him.

* * *

The medicine Imatinib is used to treat leukemia and costs 65,000 dollars for a year's supply. In India the same medicine is available for 2,500 dollars a year, because the pharma company could not patent it there.

* * *

During the expansion of the railway network in Uganda, an incredible incident occurred. Two Tsavo lions repeatedly killed workers during night and slowed the construction progress. About 135 people died this way.

* * *

Short female car drivers have the highest likelihood of being killed by the cars airbag due to their close distance to the steering wheel.

* * *

Gnats are especially attracted by people with blood type O.

* * *

Every year, about 4 million cats are consumed as delicacies in China.

* * *

The deaf cannot get seasick.

* * *

The "Jesus nut" is the bolt that holds the rotor blades of a helicopter together. The name of the bolt was given by its importance. When it breaks, only a prayer to Jesus helps one to survive.

* * *

There is actually a website about Barney Stinson's fake character "Lorenzo von Matterhorn" from "How I Met Your Mother": www.lorenzovonmatterhorn.com.

* * *

Although Beethoven has a song called "Fuer Elise", historians have proven that he did not know an Elise.

* * *

In 1938, Adolf Hitler was Time Magazine's "Person of the Year".

* * *

If McDonald's was its own country, it would be the 90th biggest economy in the world.

* * *

The actor Mark Wahlberg was suspended from school after just a few years and therefore never finished it. To be a shining example to his kids, he catched up in his high school diploma in the age of 42.

* * *

If you watch all Saw movies at once, it will take you 666 minutes.

* * *

At the age of 17, young Pattie Mellette got pregnant and was forced to have an abortion by her parents. She refused. Her child is Justin Bieber.

* * *

The Make-A-Wish-Foundation collects money to fulfil the dreams of seriously ill children.

* * *

James Harrison is a record holder in blood donations. He donated his blood over 1,000 times.

* * *

To find out whether a female is capable of mating, male giraffes beat their heads on the female's belly until they urinate. The male can determine the female's fertility by the smell of her urine.

* * *

In the U.S., the probability of suicide is twice the rate of an assassination by a third party.

* * *

A study showed that the sight of meat has a soothing effect on men.

* * *

The indents on a golf ball are called "dimples".

* * *

According to the Global Age Watch Index 2014, Germany is the third best country on earth after Sweden and Norway, to live as long as possible.

* * *

School grades are just as valuable as an indicator of intelligence as age is for personal maturity.

* * *

Four out of five people sing in the car.

* * *

By law, cars are prohibited on Mackinac Island in Michigan since 1898. Inhabitants use horses instead.

* * *

Twelve newborn babies are given to false parents every day.

* * *

Pablo Escobar - the world's biggest drug lord - had so much cash that he had to spend 2,500 dollars a month on rubber bands that held his money together.

* * *

Jonah Falcon has the biggest penis in the world. It has a length of almost 14 inches.

* * *

An American married the Eiffel Tower in 2007.

* * *

If you could drive directly to the moon by car at a speed of 80 miles per hour, it would take about four months to reach it.

* * *

In preparation for his role as Walter White in "Breaking Bad" Bryan Cranston was taught by the DEA how to make meth.

* * *

The Hard Rock Cafe T-shirts are the world's best-selling T-shirts.

* * *

In Ukraine there is a 1,000 feet deep salt mine, which is used in the treatment of respiratory diseases. Due to the high salt content, there are fewer bacteria in the air than compared to the most sterile rooms of a hospital.

* * *

Thanks to collaboration with Twitter, every public tweet sent in the U.S., is digitally archived in the Library of Congress.

* * *

Russian man, Valery Spiridonov is alleged to be the first human to receive a head transplant. His head will be grafted onto another body.

* * *

In Australia, a hog stole 18 beers from a camping site, got drunk and then tried to attack a cow.

* * *

Before the word "Zombie" became a common term, Marvel had rights to the word.

* * *

Sony has developed a refrigerator which exclusively is opened while smiling.

* * *

Adult cats exclusively meow to communicate with humans.

* * *

All books in Dumbledore's library in the Harry Potter films are actually telephone books, which have been remodeled to look like old books.

* * *

Once, Charlie Chaplin took part in a Charlie Chaplin imitator contest and came in third place.

* * *

The clitoris has more than 8,000 nerve endings, while the penis just has 4,000.

* * *

In Stockholm, Sweden, there is speed camera which raffles the income from speeding tickets among those who drive at the correct speed.

* * *

Babies are born with 300 bones. In adulthood this number decreases to 206.

* * *

About 99 percent of all Estonians have blue eyes.

* * *

The abbreviation "X-Mas" for Christmas can be traced back to the ancient Greeks. The X stands for the Greek letter "Chi" which used to be the abbreviation for the word Christ.

* * *

On Jupiter and Saturn it rains diamonds.

* * *

Nowadays, 82 percent of young people do not ring doors anymore, but send a message that they have arrived and wait outside the door.

* * *

Blind people have nightmares, and have them four times more often than normal seeing people do.

* * *

The Italian chocolate brand "Italo Suisse" changed its name in 2013 to "Isis". One year later it had to change it again because of the rise of the terror organization.

* * *

Multimillionaire Forrest Fenn, hid a treasure worth two million dollars in the Rocky Mountains. In order to find it, you have to solve a number of puzzles. Until today, nobody has found the treasure.

* * *

In summer the Eiffel Tower is 5.9 inches higher than in winter.

* * *

Neptune, Saturn and Venus are the names of three seaside resorts in Romania.

* * *

Marvel originally was named "Timely Comics".

* * *

50,000 people die a year in the U.S. from the effects of passive smoking

* * *

Just five percent of all babies suck their left thumb. The remaining 95 percent use their right one.

* * *

In 2008, a Brazilian tied 1,000 balloons to a chair and flew into the air. Two weeks later his corpse was found in the sea.

* * *

The Audi brand name e-tron means "pile of shit" in French.

* * *

Hulk originally was meant to be a grey monster but as the printing works had problems to always use the identical shade of grey, the creators decided to turn Hulk green.

* * *

The likelihood of getting bitten by a human in New York is higher than the likelihood of getting bitten by a shark in the sea.

* * *

The maximum speed of a T.Rex was slower than the average sprinting speed of a human.

* * *

On June 30th, 2015, there was a leap second. One second was added to the last minute of this day.

* * *

The Australian prisoner Joseph Bolitho Johns broke out of prison so often that the police built a special prison cell for him. He also broke out of this.

* * *

Like humans, ducks have different accents.

* * *

The earth is the only planet in our solar system, that is not named after a god.

* * *

Django Unchained was the first movie in sixteen years in which Leonardo DiCaprio wasn't the highest paid actor on set.

* * *

When your fingers swell from being underwater too long, it is because of an evolutionary trait of your nervous system. The fingers swell so as to provide more grip in wet conditions.

* * *

Astronauts in the ISS can witness 15 sunrises and 15 sunsets a day.

* * *

It takes eight minutes and 17 seconds until the light from the sun reaches the earth.

* * *

The Bonobo Kanzi monkey is able to make its own bonfire and cook its food in it.

* * *

Leonardo DiCaprio was named after Leonardo da Vinci. His mother was looking at a drawing by the artist in a museum, when she felt young Leonardo move for the first time.

* * *

The astronomer Eugene Shoemaker is the only human whose ash was transported to the moon after his death.

* * *

The embryos of the Sandtiger shark fight each other in the mother's womb. The surviving embryo will ultimately be born.

* * *

Google uses camels with a camera attached in the desert to get images for Google Street View.

* * *

Schwuugle describes itself as "the gay search engine".

* * *

Your hearing is worse when you are well fed.

* * *

The country code of Russia is 007.

* * *

Nearly 65 percent of all autistic people are left-handed.

* * *

Goats have rectangular pupils.

* * *

In Cambodia you can buy pizzas with marijuana as a topping. It is called Happy Pizza.

* * *

Female lions carry out 90 percent of the lion's hunting activities.

* * *

Human blood contains about 0.2 milligrams of gold.

* * *

Two of the richest men in the world - Bill Gates and Warren Buffet - officially stated that they will donate 90 percent of their assets when they pass away.

* * *

Scientists of Stanford University observed that a walk can increase people's creativity by up to 60 percent.

* * *

When crying tears of joy, the first one mainly comes from the right eye, while the first tear of sorrow mostly comes from the left.

* * *

The average rent for a one room apartment in Manhattan is 3,400 dollars.

* * *

Ten percent of all car accidents are caused by being distracted, for example when writing an SMS.

* * *

The Towers of the World Trade Centre had their own zip code: 10048 New York.

* * *

The book "Everything men know about woman" consists of 100 blank pages.

* * *

Originally, Mickey Mouse was called Mortimer Mouse.

* * *

The most common cause of death in Germany for men and women is coronary heart disease.

* * *

Frequent sex increases the growth of brain cells.

* * *

It only takes one drop of engine oil to contaminate more than 25 liters of water.

* * *

If 57 people are gathered in one room, the likelihood of two of the people having their birthday on the same day, is about 99 percent.

* * *

On average, a person farts 14 times a day.

* * *

Only five percent of all humans have red hair.

* * *

Sound spreads through steel about 15 times faster than through air.

* * *

The Marvel superhero Northstar, a French-Canadian mutant, was the first gay superhero in the world.

* * *

When we talk to somebody we like, our voice changes.

* * *

"May I have a large container of coffee". If you count the number of letters of every word in this sentence you get a good approximation for pi.

* * *

Walter Summerford was struck by lightning in his life three times. After he died, his gravestone was also struck by lightning.

* * *

Nothing is an uninhabited town in the U.S. state of Arizona. There is nothing but a gas station and a garage.

* * *

The word "blood" is mentioned at least once in every Shakespeare piece.

* * *

In 2014 a woman was saved from her burning house. She then realized she had forgot her mobile phone in the house, ran back into her home and died.

* * *

In 1867 the USA bought Alaska from Russia for just 7.2 million dollars.

* * *

The entire human population could live in New Zealand, and the population density would still be lower than that of Manhattan in New York.

* * *

In 1925, Coca-Cola published a key pendant in the shape of a swastika.

* * *

To avoid baggage fees, a man from China wore 70 items of clothing on his body.

* * *

City birds are now integrating cigarette stubs into their nests as they have recognized that these are effective against insects.

* * *

The oldest bridge in France is called "Pont Neuf".
Translated it means "New Bridge".

* * *

In Newfoundland (Canada) there is a city called Dildo.

* * *

An ostrich can run a marathon in less than 60 minutes.

* * *

The world record for the most push-ups in one day is
46,001.

* * *

From 1912 to 1948 architecture was an Olympic discipline.

* * *

The human brain consumes about 20 percent of the body's
total energy.

* * *

An average vagina is three to four inches deep and can
increase by up to 200 percent when the woman is aroused.

* * *

The Lily actress Alyson Hannigan from "How I Met Your
Mother" is married to Alexis Dennis in real life, the actor
of news reader Sandy Rivers.

* * *

The blue whale is the loudest animal on earth. Its cries can be heard from a distance of 373 miles.

* * *

Araucana chickens are also referred to as Easter egg chickens, because their eggs can be blue, green, red or brown.

* * *

The actress Mila Kunis suffers from heterochromia iridum. So she has two different eye colors.

* * *

Babies are not able to taste salt until they are four months old.

* * *

Nepal is the only country in the world that does not have a rectangular flag.

* * *

There are so many languages in the world that it is not known how many there currently are. Scientists believe that there are more than 6,500 to 7,000 different languages.

* * *

A behavioral study came to the conclusion that brunette women are perceived as more intelligent by their peers than women with other hair colors.

* * *

When the ninth symphony came out, Beethoven had already become deaf and could not hear it anymore.

* * *

Besides humans, ants and bees are the only animals to wage war against members of the same species.

* * *

In almost all of his songs, Lenny Kravitz does not only sing, but also plays all instruments in a recording studio.

* * *

Adolescents are increasingly suffering from sleep deprivation. The reason for this is, among other things, the early start of school.

* * *

There is more bacteria on your own skin then there are living people in the world.

* * *

In the last 150 years, the average body size of a human has increased by four inches.

* * *

In France there is a village named "Pussy".

* * *

The Batman series from the 1960s was known for its educational themes. The viewers were invited to fasten their seatbelts in the car, do homework, drink milk and eat healthily.

* * *

The more educated a couple is, the lower the probability of divorce.

* * *

In terms of the level of medical accuracy, Scrubs is the best medical television series in the world.

* * *

A study came to the conclusion that female students, who are perceived as attractive by their fellow male students, achieve better grades.

* * *

A U.S. court had to decide if the X-men are humans or not. In the US, imported dolls representing human beings are subject to a higher tax than other toys. As of this a toy manufacturer sued for a declaration that the action figures did not represent human beings to pay lower taxes.

* * *

If you dissolve Viagra in water and give it to your plants, they remain fresh up to a week longer.

* * *

The Jewish population is only 0.2 percent, yet 20 percent of all Nobel prizes have been awarded to people of the Jewish faith.

* * *

The largest hydrogen bomb that has been detonated caused such a big shock wave that it could still be measured after the third circumnavigation of the globe.

* * *

In Alaska there is a sand desert with dunes up to 160 feet high.

* * *

Human fingers are so sensitive that they can feel objects of 13 nanometers in size. This means that if one finger was the size of the earth, it could feel the difference between a house and a car.

* * *

Skateboard professional Tony Hawk has an IQ of 144.

* * *

Paparazzi is Italian and can be translated to "annoying mosquitoes".

* * *

Sharks were on the earth before trees existed.

* * *

In third world countries, residents can access Wikipedia via their smartphone without using their data. The "Wikipedia Zero" campaign is already available in 34 countries.

* * *

The sun is actually white. But our atmosphere makes it look yellowish to us.

* * *

About 80 percent of people breathe exclusively through one nostril. Which nostril is used by the body varies approximately every 2.5 hours. While the other nostril is not being used for breathing, the body cleans it.

* * *

One of the founders of the DNA structure - James Watson - was forced to sell his Nobel Prize in 2014 due to financial problems. He received 4.1 million dollars and the buyer gave him the Nobel Prize back afterwards.

* * *

Statistically, most cars are stolen on New Year's Day.

* * *

The Amazon is home to pink dolphins.

* * *

To keep up with speedsters, the police of Dubai are equipped with Ferraris and Lamborghinis.

* * *

It is assumed that cats are responsible for the extinction of several animal species.

* * *

The full name of Yoshi is T. Yoshisaur Munchakoopas.

* * *

In Paris there is only one stop sign.

* * *

For every episode of "The Simpsons" the producers needed six to nine months.

* * *

Terminator 2, The Silence of the Lambs, The Beauty and the Beast and the Prince of Bel Air are closer in time to the moon landing than on today's date.

* * *

Bodies transported by an airplane are denoted by "HUGO" for "Human Gone".

* * *

In Mumbai you can take out insurance against dodging paying of fares.

* * *

A Scottish study found that most heart attacks happen on a Monday.

* * *

Russia has more land mass than Pluto.

* * *

An adult oyster can clean and filter up to 190 liters of water per day.

* * *

In 1923, a dead rider finished first in a horse race in New York. The rider suffered a heart attack during the race and the horse carried the dead body to the finishing line.

* * *

In the Trevi Fountain in Rome 3,000 Euros is thrown in by tourists every day.

* * *

Cats have 32 muscles to move their ears. In comparison, humans only have six muscles in their ears.

* * *

McDonald's is the biggest customer of Coca Cola.

* * *

People who laugh more frequently, live a longer life.

* * *

In 2011, scientists flew 100 paper planes from a height of 23 miles above Germany. Some of these paper planes have been found in Canada, USA, Australia and South America.

* * *

From 200 decibels, music can be fatal, because then the air vesicles in your lung can burst.

* * *

Bruce Lee was a gifted dancer. He won the Cha-Cha Championship in Hong Kong in 1958.

* * *

In Japan, people believe that one's blood type affects one's personality. For this reason, the Japanese version of Facebook has a drop-down menu for one's blood type.

* * *

The likelihood of dying in your cab on the way to the airport is higher than to die on your flight.

* * *

People in Norway who own electric cars, are allowed to park everywhere for free, do not have to pay for the ferryboat and can drive in the bus lane.

* * *

The heart of a shrimp is located in its head.

* * *

Einstein was asked what it was like to be the smartest guy in the world, he answered "I don't know, ask Nikola Tesla".

* * *

One pound of muscles burns 16,300 calories per year.

* * *

In 2014, Red Bull spent a billion dollars on marketing, but only 600 million dollars on the production of beverages.

* * *

The former U.S. Marine soldier Guy Gabaldon was able to catch about 800 Japanese soldiers during World War Two.
The Japanese soldiers were hiding in a cave and Guy Gabaldon sneaked in. He convinced them that their cave was surrounded. After everyone was handcuffed he called for support.

* * *

Most suicides happen on Mondays.

* * *

In Italy, a man left his cat an inheritance of about ten million Euros.

* * *

When being asked for his IQ, Stephen Hawking answered: "I have no idea. People who boast about their IQ are losers"

* * *

The role of John McClane in "Die Hard" actually went to Arnold Schwarzenegger - however he declined the role.

* * *

The molecule Penguinone got its name because of its chemical structure which resembles a penguin.

* * *

Only two percent of all people have green eyes.

* * *

Arnold Schwarzenegger was meant to play the role of Kyle
Reese in the movie "Terminator".

* * *

The WWF chose a panda for its logo, in order to save
print costs and to set a sign.

* * *

The Swedish word for stepmother is "Bonusmamma".

* * *

Parkinson's Law describes the fact that an employee needs
as much time for a task as he has available for it.

* * *

About 31 percent of Germany's surface is covered by
forest.

* * *

Robert Lane named his two sons "Winner" and "Loser".
Winner Lane turned criminal, while Loser Lane had a
successful career at the NYPD.

* * *

The human brain needs 33 milliseconds to determine the mood of a person, from their facial expressions alone.

* * *

The human heartbeat changes when listening to music and adapts to the sound.

* * *

The first ATMs required six digits as a PIN. However, after a large number of users could not remember six digits, the PIN was reduced to four digits.

* * *

The inventor of cotton candy was also a practicing dentist.

* * *

Everyday McDonald's serves over 68 million people. This is approximately one percent of the world's population.

* * *

Hippopotami on average kill 2,900 humans per year, stags 130, ants 30, cows 22, horses 20 and sharks only five. But who would run away from a cow?

* * *

Nearly one in five Germans regularly use a laptop on the toilet.

* * *

Koala bears hug trees to cool down on hot days.

* * *

To date, it is not clear why people and other animals need sleep. There are many theories, but even experts are uncertain about their accuracy.

* * *

The maiden name of Goethe's mother was "Textor".

* * *

McDonald's earns 8.7 billion dollars a year though franchise revenue only. That is more than the gross domestic product of Mongolia.

* * *

In the last 3,000 years, there were only 268 years in which no wars occurred.

* * *

The children of the nephews of Adolf Hitler had voluntarily sterilized themselves, in order for the Hitler bloodline to become extinct.

* * *

As early as 1966 Ford released the first electric car, which had a range of more than 200 miles. A sodium-sulphur accumulator was used as a battery. After an accident in rainy weather, the hot sodium leaking from the battery mixed with water and ignited. There was a fire that was difficult to extinguish. As a result, the model was reset and sodium-sulphur batteries were no longer used in vehicles.

* * *

Gladiators in ancient Rome were exclusively fighters who fought against other humans for life and death. People fighting exclusively against animals were called "Bestiarii".

* * *

It is a long tradition in Ireland to leave a bottle of beer at the front door for Santa Claus.

* * *

About 90 percent of people won't find the the mistake in here:
A,B,C,D,E,F,G,H,I,J,K,L,M,N,O,P,Q,R,S,T,U,V,W,X,Y,Z.

* * *

The record for most passengers on an airplane was set in 1991 with 1,081 people. Two babies were born during the flight.

* * *

Monopoly was developed in 1930 in the U.S. to create a pastime for the unemployed people during the great depression.

* * *

In 1997, Microsoft employed 31,000 people worldwide, of which 21 000 already were millionaires because of their participation in the company.

* * *

McDonald's sells 75 burgers per minute.

* * *

In the United States at least one person per hour gets killed in a car accident due to drinking.

* * *

The Harvard physicist Lene Hau was successful in reducing the speed of light to 38 miles per hour.

* * *

Researchers believe that only ten percent of our seas are explored. This means we know less about our oceans than about the moon.

* * *

In order to make wolf puppies urinate, their mother has to lick their bellies with her warm tongue.

* * *

More than 250,000 millionaires live in New York.

* * *

McDonald's also delivers its food - in at least 18 countries around the world.

* * *

Dubai has an indoor ski center.

* * *

Since 1944, Iceland does not have its own army, and have not been attacked by other countries since.

* * *

In 2012 about 37 percent of Italians had never used the Internet.

* * *

Many different bacteria are located in a woman's vagina. Much of those bacteria are also found in yogurt.

* * *

When rebels stormed the home of Muammar al-Gaddafi, they discovered a photo album with pictures of the former U.S. Secretary of State Condoleezza Rice.

* * *

All scenes of the children of Ted Mosby in "How I Met Your Mother" were shot during the first season.

* * *

The storming of the Bastille was mainly symbolic, at the time there were only nine prisoners who were subsequently freed.

* * *

In India, forest workers wear masks with a picture of a human face on their back of the heads so that they are not attacked by tigers.

* * *

Most people are born in August.

* * *

During the Second World War a special event was held in a news magazine. Two soldiers were betting who would be the first to kill 100 enemy soldiers with a sword. Both died before they could win the competition.

* * *

In the Turkish village Halfeti, completely black roses grow each summer.

* * *

Based on an interview, Pope Francis watched television for the last time on the 15 July 1990.

* * *

Washing your hands regularly with soap and water is a sufficiently protective mechanism against the Ebola virus.

* * *

Michael Jackson was negotiating to buy Marvel.

* * *

In Australia, the cheapest wine is cheaper than the cheapest bottle of water.

* * *

In Singapore, it is forbidden to chew gum. Only a few people are allowed to do so for medical reasons.

* * *

On average a spacesuit costs eleven million dollars.

* * *

Our blood accounts for seven percent of our body weight.

* * *

In 1952 Albert Einstein received the offer to become President of Israel. He refused.

* * *

According to his driving license, Spongebob was born on July 14, 1986.

* * *

In 1994 a man was arrested in Los Angeles for scaring elderly people. He dressed himself as the grim reaper and looked inside the windows of the elderly.

* * *

In the U.S. most movies are released on Independence Day. Conversely, the movie "Independence Day" was released a week prior to Independence Day.

* * *

Eminem repeated the ninth grade - three times.

* * *

Adrian Carton de Wiart fought in both World Wars and he was shot in his head, his leg, his hips and his ear. He also survived a plane crash and when the doctors were unwilling to amputate two of his fingers, he bit them off. When he was later asked about his time during the war he replied "I had enjoyed the war".

* * *

The explosion of a modern nuclear atomic bomb in London would produce such a large pressure wave that glass panes in Berlin would also shatter.

* * *

Flipper was played by five different dolphins.

* * *

In 1983 Marvel released a comic series called "Spider-Pig". The main character was "Peter Porker".

* * *

The longest prison sentence a man ever received was 384,912 years. The sentence was received by a 22 year old postman, who had not delivered over 42,000 letters.

* * *

The increased use of the drug "Sumatriptan" can lead to a green coloration of the blood.

* * *

If the earth were as large as a sand grain, the sun would be as large as an orange.

* * *

In the British Army only soldiers ranked "Pioneer Sergeant" are allowed to have a beard.

* * *

The highest temperature ever measured in a human body was 115.7 degrees Fahrenheit.

* * *

Nutella was invented during World War II, when an Italian soldier mixed chocolate with hazelnut to stretch his food ration.

* * *

A hug lasting more than 20 seconds releases so much oxytocin that we begin to trust the other person more.

* * *

Yellow teeth are more robust than white teeth.

* * *

When Mario had his first act in Donkey Kong in 1981, his name was "Jumpman".

* * *

It takes about 100,000 years for the sun's energy to penetrate out from the core of the sun to the outermost layer and only eight minutes until it reaches the earth.

* * *

It is estimated that 7,000 people die every year because the handwriting of the treating doctor was not legible.

* * *

With total assets of 1.5 billion dollars, Snapchat founder Evan Spiegel is the world's youngest billionaire.

* * *

Before "James Bond" actor Daniel Craig became a professional actor, he could not afford to pay his rent. Because of this he often slept on park benches.

* * *

The London Underground now makes more profit by selling its popular underground maps than it does operating the subway.

* * *

After Tupac's death, his best friends mixed his ashes with marijuana and smoked it.

* * *

Made in the USA
San Bernardino, CA
15 March 2018